American
Indian
Needlepoint
Workbook

American Indian Needlepoint Workbook

Margaret Boyles

BASED ON MATERIAL BY W. BEN HUNT AND
J. F. "BUCK" BURSHEARS

Collier Books

A Division of Macmillan Publishing Co., Inc., New York

Collier Macmillan Publishers, London

Macmillan Publishing Co., Inc.
866 Third Avenue, New York, N.Y. 10022
Collier Macmillan Canada, Ltd.

Library of Congress Cataloging in Publication Data
Boyles, Margaret.
    American Indian needlepoint workbook.

    ''Based on material by W. Ben Hunt and Buck Burshears.''
    Includes index.
    1. Canvas embroidery—Patterns. 2. Indians of
North America—Textile industry and fabrics.
I. Title.
TT778.C3B66 1975   746.4'4   75-20417
ISBN 0-02-011160-6

First Collier Books Edition 1976

PRINTED IN THE UNITED STATES OF AMERICA

Acknowledgments

My sincere thanks to W. Ben Hunt and to J. F. Burshears for their knowledge and understanding of American Indian beadwork and for allowing the use of their material in this book. Also, my thanks and appreciation to the staff at Macmillan who designed, art directed, and produced it.

But, most of all, I'd like to thank the American Indian craftsmen and artists who developed the original tribal designs. Their work was an inspiration to their people and to everyone who glories in the honest and direct use of color, texture, and symbolism in art.

Margaret Boyles

Contents

This Eskimo girl's costume comes from Greenland, a country rich in patterns adaptable for needle-point. Note the small diamond bands on the sleeves; they can be used for narrow borders, belts, or any other strip design. (Photo courtesy of the Museum of the American Indian, Heye Foundation, New York)

Introduction

The American Indians have been decorating their clothing with colorful designs since the first Indian ventured onto these continents from his original home in Asia.

Each tribe used what was available to make their designs. Some used beads made out of seeds, shells, claws, bones, and stones; others, like the plains and woodland Indians, used porcupine quills which they dyed various colors. With the discovery of America and the arrival of settlers, traders found their stocks of glass beads readily accepted in trade for furs. As the fur traders prospered, trading expeditions went deeper and deeper into the country, and they introduced the European seed bead. The Indians used the seed beads in place of the quills or in combination with them. The quillwork designs easily lent themselves to this combination. After the missionaries arrived, the lake Indians adopted the floral patterns which adorned the clerical vestments.

Many designs can be easily recognized as belonging to specific tribes. The designs of the lake Indians, for example, were often flowered; those of the Sioux or plains Indians were geometric, and the Blackfoot and northern plains Indians had massive geometrical designs. Some tribes applied animal pictures to their vests and bandoleers. For pure beauty of geometrical design, few, if any, excelled the Apache. And many people can recognize with ease the artistry the Navajos expressed in their rugs.

The following pages are made up of designs collected from many parts of the United States. Several are from the private collection of J. F. Burshears, others come from the Smithsonian Institution, Washington, D.C.; the Field Museum of Natural History, Chicago, Illinois; the Jefferson Memorial, St. Louis, Missouri; The American Indian

Museum, New York, New York; and pieces collected by the Koshare Indian Dancers of La Junta, Colorado.

Of the many thousands of designs available these are just a few, but they give a cross-section of the arts of the different tribes. When you plan your projects, don't hesitate to mix the patterns of one tribe with those of another. The Indians were great traders, and it would not be unusual to find an Indian, like the Pueblos of New Mexico, thousands of miles away, wearing a breechcloth and belt with the floral designs of the northern Ojibwa.

1 Adapting Indian beadwork to needlepoint

Loomed beadwork

Indian beaded designs fall into two categories—loomed and appliquéd or free designs. Both are readily adaptable to needlepoint as well as other embroidery forms.

The loomed designs are ideal as needlepoint patterns because they can be interpreted using one needlepoint stitch for each bead. Thus, all the designs on pages 24 to 35 are versatile needlepoint charts, ready for you to use. Most of these are band patterns which can be made into belts, bracelets, frames, borders, book marks, or bell pulls—anywhere you'd want to use a band pattern. The designs, however, are not limited to only long, narrow projects as those listed. They can be combined and enlarged to make larger pieces as shown by the finished needlepoint illustrations. Examination of these pieces will give you some ideas of the many ways the Indian patterns can be used.

Strip designs can be widened simply by adding rows of plain background or stripes to the edges. You can also enlarge the designs without losing the original feeling. The accompanying drawing shows a Sioux motif enlarged from a piece 39 rows wide by 30 rows in length to one which measures 49 by 35. This was achieved by adding those squares marked with an "x." This same method can be applied to most of the designs.

Square pieces can be put together by repeating one strip several times as was done in the Blue-Brown Sioux and the Sioux Geometric pillows. Opening up a design, as

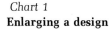

Chart 1
Enlarging a design

in the lake Indian pillow, makes a square panel as does combining many different strips in one-piece ribbon fashion as in the Floral Ribbon pillow.

Some of the designs lend themselves to natural and attractive combinations. The Sioux Mountain-Lake-Rainbow pillow and bell pull shown on page 36 use three Sioux symbols without any changes in the basic designs shown on the bead charts (see page 25).

Don't be afraid to combine the symbols of different tribes; the Indians traded designs freely, and it was common to find widely separated tribes combining traded patterns with their own. If you plan carefully, the variety of designs that can be put together from the charts in this book is unlimited. Note the lake Indian pillow; it combines floral abstracts with a border adaptation from a Sioux armband. Color and scale tie the two together into a pleasing combination.

Since a combination of designs may require some slight alterations, it is usually best to plan ahead using a sheet (or two) of graph paper. Use one square for one bead or stitch. Your chart need not be painted or colored, but you may find it helpful in visualizing the finished product.

Appliquéd beadwork

Some of the most interesting pieces in this book are examples of the appliquéd beadwork of the plains Indians. This embroidery is created by sewing strings of beads to elk- or buckskin. The western Indians used moistened sinew for stringing their beads and for sewing them onto the skins. As the sinew dried, it pulled the beads tightly against the hide giving the appearance of being imbedded. This sinew-sewed beadwork lies in ridges and has a solid feel. Later beadwork, produced after the introduction of the needle and thread, does not have this rigid feel but if done properly has the same appearance. These free and primitive designs adapt easily to embroidery and needlepoint using the tent stitch, crewelpoint on canvas, or crewel embroidery.

The design from the Ojibwa bandoleer bag on page 64 was used for the Ojibwa pillow. Couching (see Chapter 4) has been used to capture the appearance of the sewn beadwork on the canvas; however, the design would still

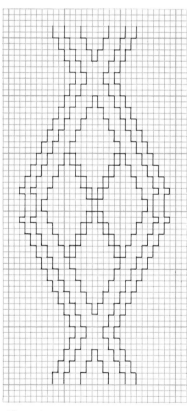

Chart 2
Diamond design from Potawatomi costume

be attractive if worked in traditional needlepoint or as crewel embroidery on linen.

Many examples of appliquéd beadwork have been included for inspiration for embroidery as well as needlepoint. All the photographs are clear enough to make copying possible. Do not worry if you are not a skilled artist; most of the charm of these pieces lies in their unsophisticated draftsmanship.

Porcupine quill embroidery

Porcupine quill embroidery was well established among the American Indians long before the first explorers arrived. We've included some here because of its beauty and because it illustrates the inventiveness of Indian women.

Although there were several methods of attaching the quills to the skins, sewing was the one most favored. A moist piece of sinew was used as thread. The tip of the strand was twisted tightly and allowed to dry forming a sharp stiff point which was used as the needle. A stone, shaped like an awl, was used to perforate the hide to allow the crude needle to pass through the surface of the skin and over the quills. Early designs in quill embroidery were primarily geometric, but later ones show European and Spanish influence.

The geometric patterns of quill embroidery work well with the upright gobelin stitch—using one stitch for each quill. The stitches themselves resemble quills, and the result is quite pleasing.

Color

The Indian's love of color is apparent in every piece of beadwork and quill embroidery and predates the coming of the explorers. Anthropological finds indicate that the Indians had crude beads very early in their history. These old beads were made of copper, quartz, magnetite, slate, turquoise, and silver as well as seeds, shells, claws, bones, horns, and stones. When the Europeans started traveling to the new world, they brought along bright-colored beads to

A beautiful example of lavish and intricate appliqué beadwork. This Potawatomi costume, worn by Donald Hopkins, is made of trade cloth. Each design can be adapted for needlepoint. The diagram on page 2 is from the leg band. (Photo courtesy of the Museum of the American Indian, Heye Foundation, New York)

use for trading. The Indians treasured these beads and worked them into glowing designs.

Most of the colors were bright—red, yellow, turquoise, blue, green, purple. The graphed charts (pages 24 to 35) show the original colors and are a good reference for proper Indian combinations. Color changes are, of course, possible but must be carefully thought out if the true Indian flavor is to be retained.

2 American Indian designs

The following photographs are of articles made by American Indians. They reflect only a small variety of the ways in which bead and quill designs were used. The American Indians used hundreds of symbols, and each garment or article was carefully decorated with traditional motifs and individual artistry.

Though most of the articles pictured here are small, the designs can be adapted to larger pieces such as rugs, spreads, chair seats, or even suitcases.

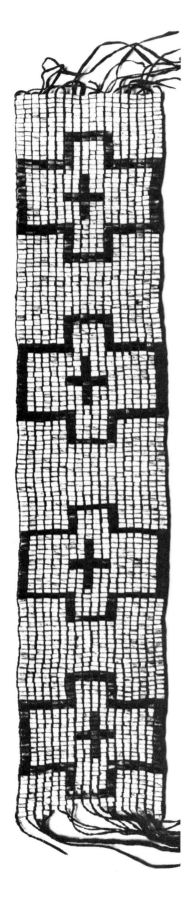

LEFT: *A simple geometric design. This 5¼ x 24½-inch wampum belt was made by a Delaware tribe now located in Pennsylvania. (Photo courtesy of the Museum of the American Indian, Heye Foundation, New York)*

ABOVE: *Detail of a quilled Iroquois pouch.*

ABOVE: *This neckband, beaded and woven on buckskin, is from the Potawatomi Indians of Pehstigo, Wisconsin. It is decorated with a shell gorget with the Underwater Panther finely etched on one side. (Photo courtesy of the Museum of the American Indian, Heye Foundation, New York)*

LEFT: *Beaded Ute pouch and shoulder sash, 28 inches long. (Photo courtesy of the Museum of the American Indian, Heye Foundation, New York)*

Two beaded shoulder guards (top: 6 x 6¾ inches; bottom: 6 x 8 inches). These designs can easily be adapted for clothing, pillows, or even a typewriter cover.

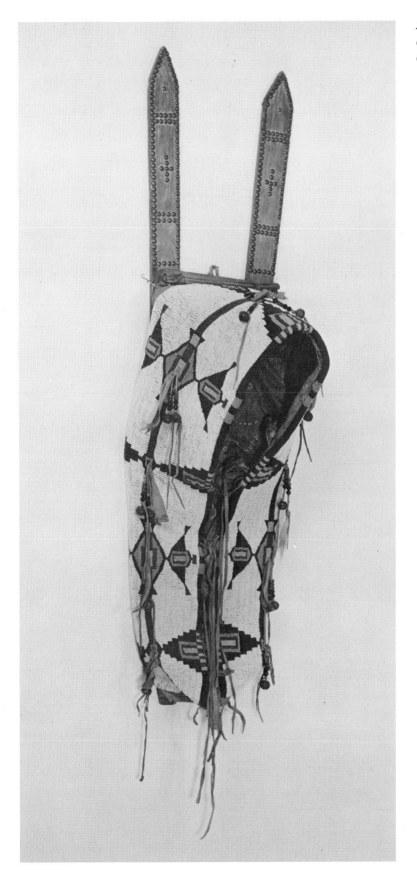

A modern baby blanket might use some of the designs from this Arapaho baby carrier.

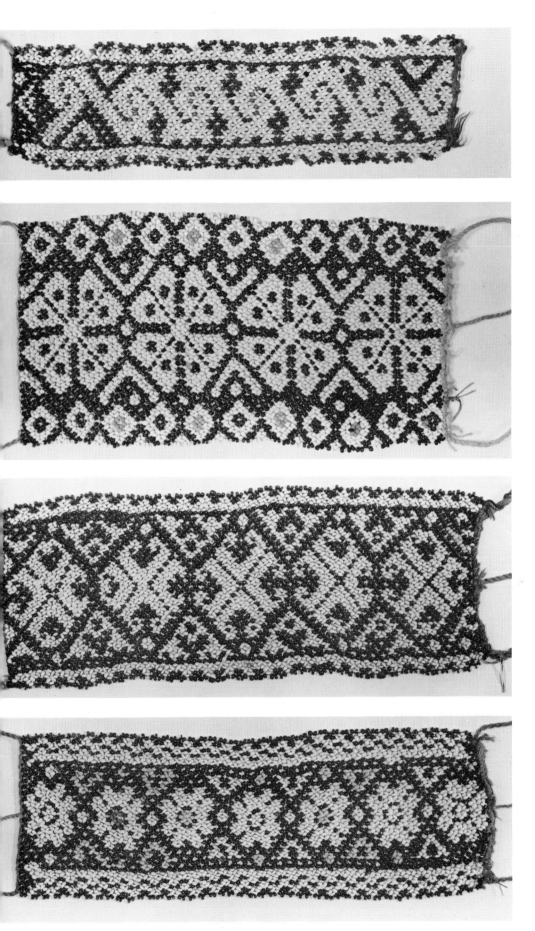

FACING PAGE: *Examples of Crow beadwork. The designs on these moccasins can be enlarged and mixed to make striking needlepoint. (Photo courtesy of the Museum of the American Indian, Heye Foundation, New York)*

LEFT: *Bracelets beaded by the Huichol Indians, Zacatecas, Mexico. They readily lend themselves as borders or strip needlepoint pieces. (Photos courtesy of the Museum of the American Indian, Heye Foundation, New York)*

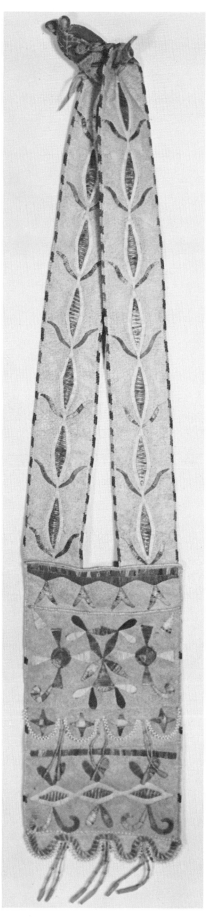

TOP LEFT: *This coat with embroidered trim gives the imaginative needle-pointer the idea of how to decorate a solid colored dress, jacket, or coat.*

BOTTOM LEFT: *An easy design to follow, this beaded bag would make an attractive tote or shopping bag. Made by the Ponca Indians of Oklahoma, this piece is about 20 inches wide. (Photo courtesy of the Museum of the American Indian, Heye Foundation, New York)*

RIGHT: *The repetition of rhythmic designs often used by American Indians is shown in this shoulder pouch.*

This elaborately beaded shoulder bag is possibly the work of a Cherokee tribesman. Under the flap is embroidered: To General Jackson from Sam Houston. (Photo courtesy of the Museum of the American Indian, Heye Foundation, New York)

TOP LEFT: *This appliquéd beadwork piece by Alaskan Indians features a central picture of an animal, a bird, and an eye.*

BOTTOM LEFT: *The use and blending of several designs is shown on this Alaskan pouch and shoulder strap. Note how the pouch design carries the strap designs.*

ABOVE: *Quillwork and beads are combined in this shirt by the Brule Sioux. It was collected in 1855 from Chief Spotted Tail. (Photo courtesy of the Museum of the American Indian, Heye Foundation, New York)*

Indian pottery is a forgotten source of many possible needlepoint designs; these three are only a small sample of their diversity. TOP RIGHT: This piece, measuring 13 inches in diameter, is from Rio de Jesus, Panama. (Photo courtesy of the Museum of the American Indian, Heye Foundation, New York)

A quilled birch bark wall pocket from Micmac, Maine. The best needlepoint stitch for imitating quillwork is a simple long one. (Photo courtesy of the Museum of the American Indian, Heye Foundation, New York)

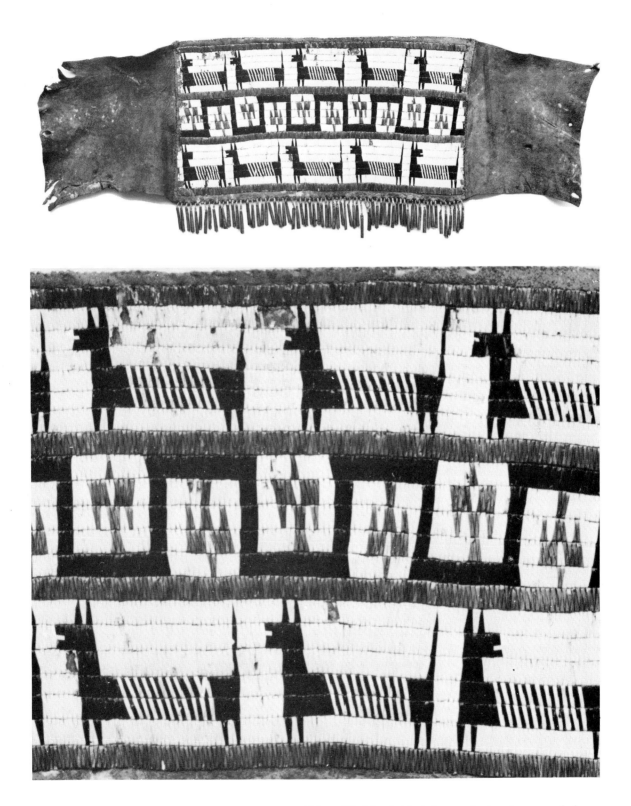

This quilled buckskin baby carrier band was made by a Delaware Indian. The detail is shown in the photo below it. (Photo courtesy of the Museum of the American Indian, Heye Foundation, New York)

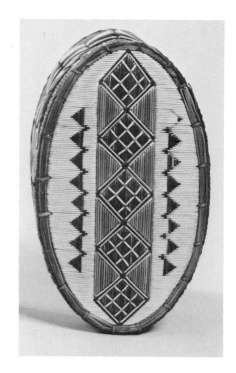

Some beautiful examples of quill designs that can easily be adapted to canvas embroidery. Notice the strong resemblance to Bargello needlepoint.

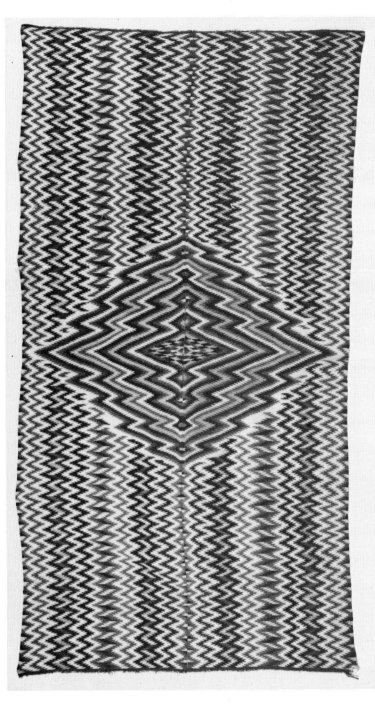

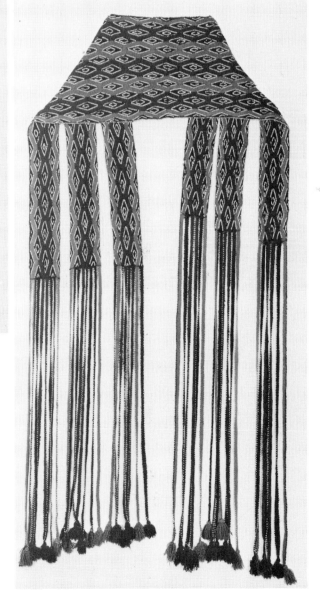

ABOVE: *The central pattern of this woven piece can be used for a Bargello pillow.*
RIGHT: *Small diamonds float on colored bands on this piece. Tassel trimming is appropriate with any American Indian design.*

Another design idea from Indian work, a figure outline on a solid background.

A design which can be used alone or in a strip.

3 Projects and charts of tribal designs

The following pages are photographs of the projects that appear in Chapter 7 and the color charts of American Indian designs. The projects were all made from the designs shown. You can select the pattern you like and, using either the color charts here or your own, use the basic stitches to make your project.

Apache and Ute designs: The top three bands are from belts (and represent half a belt), the middle design is from an Apache choker (worn by girls in their puberty ceremonials), the bottom three designs are from the Towaoc Ute Reservation and are excellent examples of Ute geometric designs.

24

Sioux designs: This collection of geometric designs shows various Sioux symbols such as the star, four winds, turtle, rainbow (second from bottom), and the mountain and lake design (bottom band).

25

Sioux designs: This collection of beadwork was taken from belts, arm bands, and leg bands.

Sioux and Cheyenne designs: These geometric designs are ideal for any border or strip design; the Utes used similar designs for hatbands.

Ute, Sioux, and Cheyenne designs: The tepee and mountain symbols shown here are from headdress brow bands.

Lake Indian designs: The floral (top band) and the grape (second from bottom band) designs show the influence of the Europeans, while the geometric pattern (middle band) strongly resembles a rattlesnake.

This montage is a collection of designs already shown. They are repeated in this manner to show how large designs can be reduced to meet one's needs without losing the motif and beauty of the original.

Ute designs: These floral designs are the most popular ones made by
the Utes. With the exception of the middle band (a butterfly symbol),
these examples are very realistic.

Ojibwa and Ute designs: All of these designs are Ute except for the band on the far left which is an Ojibwa floral abstraction.

Blackfoot designs: These large designs and their masses of solid colors are from bags and cradlebands.

Sioux designs: These designs are from pipe-bags and saddlebags; each is a different way of symbolizing the four winds.

*These designs were taken from shirts and arm strips. The first two (left)
are Ogallala Sioux, the third (left) is Apache, and the others are Sioux.*

UPPER LEFT: *Floral Ribbon Pillow;*
ABOVE LEFT AND RIGHT: *Sioux
Mountain-Lake-Rainbow Pillow and
Bell Pull;* LEFT: *Ojibwa Pillow*

TOP,: *Acoma Pillow;* ABOVE
LEFT: *Blue-Brown Sioux Pillow;*
ABOVE RIGHT: *Sioux Saddlebag Pillow;*
RIGHT: *Sioux Geometric Pillow*

ABOVE: *Navajo Pillow;* RIGHT: *Lake Indian Pillow*

4　Needlepoint basics

Needlepoint is embroidery on a canvas of cotton or linen threads woven to form a regular open mesh. There are several types of canvas which are used universally; these are penelope, mono, and the new interlocking mono. All are available in white and ecru. Color does not affect the quality, but should be considered. When working with light- or bright-colored yarns, a white canvas is advisable.

Penelope canvas, often called double mesh, is woven with two horizontal and two vertical threads forming each

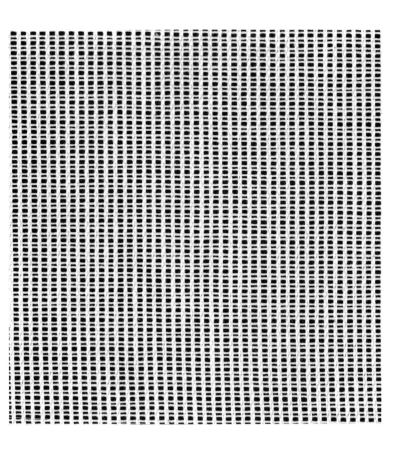

Penelope canvas

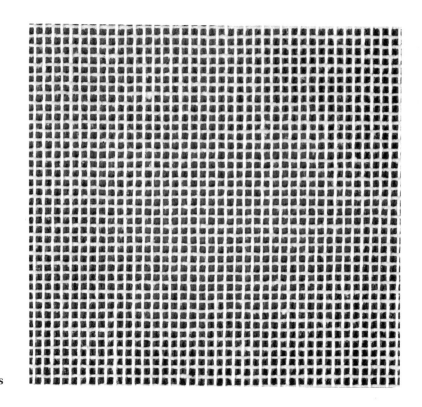

Mono canvas

mesh. This double weave and the way the threads interlock make it a very stable and superior canvas. Most stitches can be worked on penelope, and the mesh can be split to allow both petit point and gros point to be used in the same piece.

As its name implies, mono, or uni, canvas is woven with only one horizontal and one vertical thread. This creates spaces that are larger than those of penelope and makes the stitches easier to see while the work is in progress.

Interlocking mono canvas is a new development combining the advantages of penelope with those of mono. Like penelope, it is woven of double threads twisted at each intersection to form a good stable canvas, but the threads are given an extra twist between mesh that holds them together to enlarge the spaces into mono's easy-to-see weave.

Quality of canvas is very important. Shop carefully and examine the canvas before it is cut. Make certain that there are no tied threads or threads of uneven thickness. The surface of the canvas should be smooth to the hand. The threads should be round; an inferior canvas will look as if it had been pressed flat by an iron. Sizing is important to the canvas—it keeps the threads in place and preserves the shape of the canvas—but it should not be excessive. Experience will help you in knowing which canvases are sized properly, but in your first purchases you will have to rely on the salesperson. Be certain to buy the best quality.

Canvas is woven in many widths so it is best to know the measurements of your project to insure getting the width that will cut most economically. A 36-inch width is ideal for pillows since most are 14-inch square. A half-yard of this width will be sufficient for two pillows. When planning, always allow two inches on all sides for the unworked borders. Do not scrimp on this important point. The borders help keep the needlepoint in shape and are necessary in blocking.

Yarns

The two yarns most generally accepted as best for needlepoint are the traditional tapestry yarns and the newer Persian yarns. Both are offered in an enticing array of colors and shades.

The Persian yarns are sold in convenient small skeins. The yarn is three-ply—each strand is made of three fine strands twisted lightly into one—and can be easily separated, making it appropriate for a variety of canvas sizes. One strand, or ply, is used for petit point, two for No. 14 canvas, all three for No. 10 canvas. This is a fine, long-wearing wool yarn which is suitable for most needlepoint projects. Brands vary, but many are treated to be moth resistant and colorfast. Check individual labels carefully for this information.

Traditional tapestry yarn is a tightly twisted yarn with a smooth finish. It has excellent wearing qualities and is easy to use. It is generally an imported yarn, both moth-proofed and light resistant. Wool is a favorite fiber for tapestry yarns, but new ones are available in synthetics and in blends of artificial fibers and wool.

Occasionally a yarn not specifically intended for needlepoint will best fill a need for color or texture in a project. When this happens, it is perfectly permissible to use the yarn providing it is compatible with the use the finished piece will get. It should be remembered that yarns intended for hand knitting are usually spun with a soft hand and will not take the hard wear that some needlepoint receives. However, there is no reason not to incorporate knitting yarns into a picture, pillow, or fashion accessory.

Needles

A tapestry needle with rounded, blunt tip and elongated eye should be used for needlepoint. These are made in various sizes to accommodate different weights of yarn and canvas; the sizes range from a tiny 24 for petit point to a large 13 to be used on rug canvas for quickpoint. The correct needle size is important. It must be large enough to easily carry the yarn through the mesh, but not so large that it stretches the mesh out of place. The following chart is a guide for the most frequently used canvas sizes.

Canvas size	Correct needle
No. 14	Size 20
No. 12	Size 18 or 19
No. 10	Size 18
No. 7	Size 16
No. 5	Size 13

1

Two methods of threading the needle

To thread your needle using the folding method, hold the needle between the thumb and forefinger of your right hand with the eye of the needle facing you (see part 1 of diagram). Fold the yarn across the needle and pull it tightly to form a fold. Hold the fold tightly with the left hand and withdraw the needle gently. Then force the fold through the eye of the needle (part 2 of diagram).

To thread your needle by the paper method, cut a small piece of paper narrow enough to pass through the eye of the needle and about an inch long. Fold the paper as shown in part 1 of the diagram and place the cut end of the yarn in the fold. Pass the folded end of the paper through the eye of the needle (part 2 of diagram), and the yarn will be carried through easily.

2

Diagram 1 **Folding method**

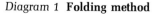

42

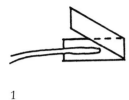

1

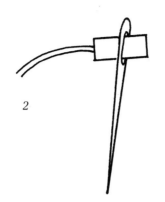

2

Diagram 2 **Paper method**

Scissors and thimble

A pair of good embroidery scissors is important. A really superior pair has smooth tapered blades and sharp tips (to aid in removing stitches). Keep the scissors in a case (to avoid damaging the piece) and with your needlepoint; try to avoid using them for other purposes which might damage or dull the blades.

The decision to use a thimble or not is really up to you. If you normally use one and can work comfortably wearing it, by all means do so. Personal preference is the only determinant.

5 Stitches

Since the Indian designs in this book are fairly complicated and involve the use of many colors, they will be most successfully worked in one of the basic tent stitches. These stitches—the continental, the half cross, and the basket weave—form the backbone of all needlepoint stitchery and are already familiar to many. Small and neat, the stitches always slant across one intersection of canvas from lower left to upper right. They fit together neatly and completely cover the canvas. Which stitch you choose depends on your plans for the finished product. Since some stitches require more yarn than others, plan ahead. The embroidered surface produced by the stitches is like the sample shown here.

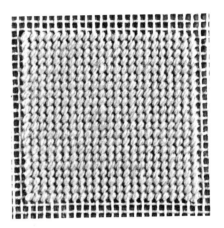

Tent stitch

The continental stitch

The versatile continental stitch is probably the most widely used needlepoint stitch and can be used for almost any project. It is easy to learn and easy to maneuver in small areas which will be important in the Indian designs. The wrong side of a canvas worked in the continental stitch reveals long diagonal threads which creates a natural padding and adds greatly to the amount of wear the piece will sustain.

You will notice, when working the continental stitch, that the canvas is pulling out of shape. This is a tendency of this particular stitch, but it can usually be corrected successfully by blocking.

The continental stitch starts in the upper right corner

Wrong side of continental stitch

of the canvas. The background rows are worked horizontally across the canvas; when you reach the left edge, turn the canvas and work the return row. The short design rows are worked in the same way; work to the edge of the design, turn the canvas around, and work the return row to the right edge of the design.

To begin the continental stitch, bring the needle up in the space for the first stitch, see Diagram 3. Leave a tail of yarn about half an inch long on the back. Hold the end in place with the index finger of the other hand and make subsequent stitches over and through it until fastened (four or five stitches). Following the diagram, take the needle across one intersection of the canvas and go down in the space numbered 2. Bring the needle to the front in the space numbered 3. When the needle goes down again at 4, note that by passing it under two threads it can be brought up at 5 in a single motion. Continue to work in this manner to the end of the row. Turn the canvas so that the top is at the bottom and work the return row following Diagram 4. Note the placement of the second row of stitches directly under those of the first row. When working the second row be careful not to split the stitches of the first when bringing the needle to the surface.

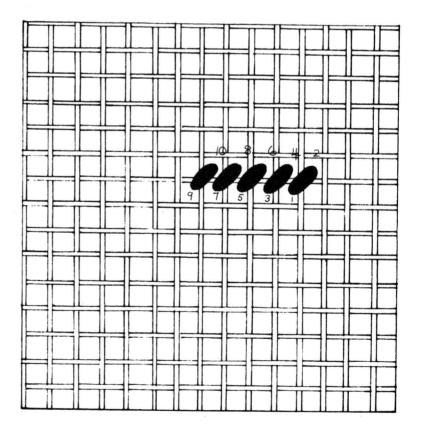

Diagram 3

Continental stitch, row 1

46

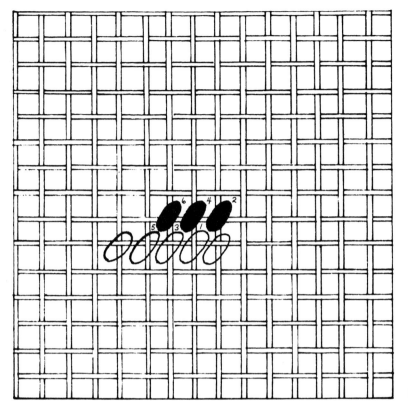

Diagram 4
Continental stitch, row 2

The basket weave stitch

Although a little harder to master than the continental stitch, the basket weave is very interesting to work; many needleworkers become so fascinated with it that they decide it is the only stitch that should ever be used.

As the illustration shows, the wrong side of the stitch has a distinctive "woven" appearance. This extra yarn gives the piece good padding which adds greatly to the wearing ability of the needlepoint. It's an excellent choice for any piece that is going to get hard wear. Another advantage of this stitch is the small amount of canvas distortion it causes; blocking is usually very easy.

The stitch is worked in diagonal rows beginning at the upper right of the canvas. The rows alternate—one row down the diagonal line, the next row up the diagonal. The key to understanding the stitch is to know that each row is one stitch longer than the preceding row.

Begin the basket weave stitch by bringing the needle up in the space for the first stitch (see Diagram 5) leaving a

Wrong side of basket weave stitch

47

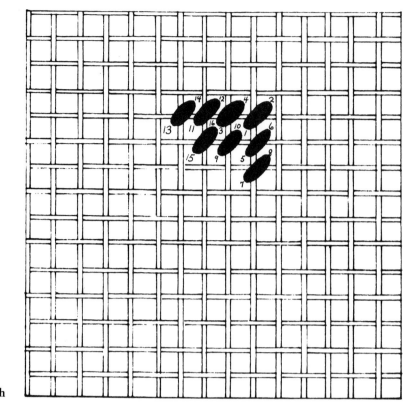

Diagram 5
Basket weave stitch

half an inch of yarn on the back of the canvas. Hold the little tail in place with the index finger of the other hand for the first few stitches working over and through it until fastened. Follow the diagram carefully for the proper order until you completely understand the stitch. Bring the needle to the front at 1. Go down at 2 across one intersection of the canvas and in the same motion pass the needle under two bars to come up at 3—these three moves are the same as the continental stitch. Take the needle down again at 4, pass it under two horizontal threads, and come up at 5. When the needle goes down at 6, row 2, which is only two stitches long, will be completed. To keep the edge straight a stitch must be placed directly under the last stitch of row 2 (the stitch made with moves 5 and 6). To do so, bring the needle up at 7. Go down at 8, passing the needle under the two vertical threads to come up at 9. Work upward, following the diagram, to complete row 3, which is three stitches long. To get you started on row 4, the diagram shows the first two moves.

When working down the slant, the needle is always in a vertical position; when working upward, the needle is always parallel to the horizontal threads. Note, also, that it is not necessary to turn the canvas to work return rows.

48

This is a big advantage when small areas are to be worked or when the project is very large and would be awkward to keep turning.

Practice the basket weave stitch on an extra piece of canvas until you become proficient and before you attempt an irregular design.

Some projects—especially those which have perfectly straight edges without support after blocking like bell pulls and rugs—should always be worked in the basket weave stitch.

The half cross-stitch

The half cross-stitch is a good all-purpose stitch that covers the canvas well if worked properly. It is a saver of yarn for, as the illustration reveals, very little yarn is placed on the wrong side of the work. The half cross-stitch requires one-fourth less yardage than either the continental or basket weave stitches. The resulting needlepoint has less bulk and does not distort the canvas too much. The half cross does not work well on mono canvas.

The half cross-stitch can be worked either horizontally or vertically. The horizontal begins in the upper left corner and continues across to the upper right corner. Following Diagram 6 (section marked "horizontal"), bring the needle up in the space for the first stitch leaving a half-inch tail of yarn. Hold the tail and work over and through it till securely fastened. Go down at 2 diagonally across the first intersection. Slide the needle under the horizontal thread and come up at 3, immediately to the right of 1. Continue in this manner to the end of the row; turn the canvas and work the return row.

Although not as frequently used as the horizontal, the vertical half cross is faster and produces plumper, more attractive stitches. The rows are worked from the lower right edge of the canvas to the top. Fasten the yarn as in the horizontal half cross and work the first row by bringing the needle up in the first space (follow the "vertical" section of Diagram 6). Go down in the space numbered 2 diagonally across one intersection of the canvas and in the same motion bring the needle to the surface at 3 by passing it under one vertical thread. Go down again at 4 and in the same motion come up at 5. Work in this manner to the top

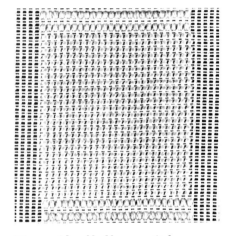

Wrong side of half cross-stitch

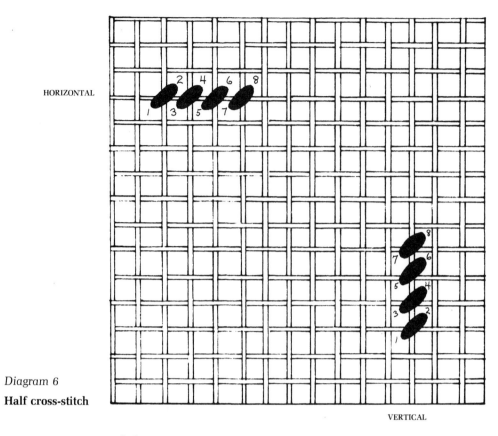

Diagram 6

Half cross-stitch

of the row. You can either end the yarn at the top and begin again at the bottom of the canvas or you can turn the canvas to work the return row.

The upright gobelin stitch

Gobelin stitch

This stitch is one of the interesting straight ones that can be worked over a varying number of threads depending on how wide a stripe of stitches is desired. The upright gobelin covers ground very quickly and is the kind of background stitch that adds texture but does not over-power the design itself. When working these vertical stitches, work with a little looser tension than normal so that the yarn can "fluff" out and cover the canvas well.

As mentioned earlier, this stitch is included because it duplicates the look of much of the Indian porcupine quill embroidery. Both the Ojibwa pillow and the detail of the armband on page 78 have been worked in upright gobelin substituting one stitch for one quill.

The stitch is an easy one. Follow the numbers in Diagram 7 for the easiest working method.

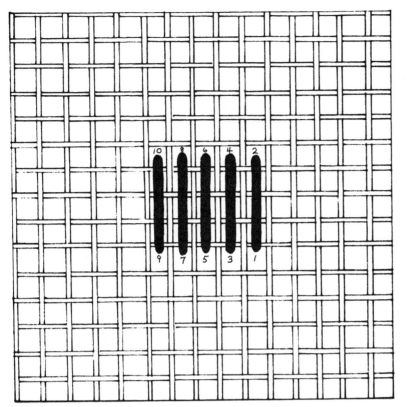

Diagram 7

Upright gobelin stitch

Couching

A couching thread can be made to do many tasks that another thread may not be able to accomplish, for the couching may be fastened at strategic points to hold the thread exactly where needed. Couching may also be used effectively to cover whole areas of pattern.

To capture the feeling of the coils of beads used in appliquéd beadwork, the couching stitch has been used for the entire design on the Ojibwa pillow (page 64). This stitch allows one to follow the curves of the design more accurately than the tent stitch and can be used to good advantage in this type of design.

Couching

Other stitches

There are literally hundreds of needlepoint stitches which space will not permit us to show. However, those looking for a reference work of stitches and stitching techniques will enjoy *Needlepoint Stitchery* by Margaret Boyles

(Macmillan). Both needlepoint and free embroidery stitches and their combinations are covered in this very thorough manual. Beginners as well as advanced students will find it a helpful volume.

6 General needlepoint instructions

Before beginning to work, plan your project carefully. The time will be well spent and will pay dividends in satisfaction later. Know in advance what the piece will be used for and plan size, color, pattern, and stitches with this in mind. Measure carefully; needlepoint cannot be stretched to a larger size nor does it shrink. Always plan to have at least two inches on each side for unworked borders. This extra canvas is useful when blocking and helps the canvas stay in shape while being worked.

The cut edges of the canvas should be covered with masking tape or encased in folded bias binding before working. This prevents the edges from fraying and eliminates the aggravation of the yarn snagging on the stiff cut threads.

If your project is of irregular shape, outline the shape on the canvas and work only that portion; keep the canvas either square or rectangular until after it has been blocked. The surplus canvas can be cut off when finishing.

Knots should be avoided at all cost. When stretched and mounted, a knot will show as a raised area and will detract from the evenness of the work. Begin and end strands of yarn by pulling them through adjacent stitches on the wrong side. Clip all ends short so they cannot tangle or be pulled through to the right side with new stitches.

It is important that the length of yarn used in the needle be correct as yarn will wear thin if carried too long. Conversely, too many short ends on the wrong side are not desirable either. Usually, the finer the canvas, the shorter the strand of yarn. For petit point, 8 to 10 inches is good; on No. 10 canvas, 14 inches is advisable; on rug canvas where the yarn will be used very quickly a much longer strand can be used.

If the yarn twists in the needle, hold the canvas so the needle can swing freely and unwind itself. Do not work with twisted yarn; it will not cover the canvas well.

It is said that a good needleworker is a good ripper. It is a mistake to leave a flaw in your work. Even though no one else may notice, it will always be obvious to you. Snip out any stitches that need to be removed and replace them with new yarn.

When you are nearly finished with your needlepoint, add your name or initials and the date. You'll find it adds interest and perhaps you will be assisting a museum in the future cataloging of an heirloom.

It is best to buy sufficient quantities of yarn to complete each color to insure that all are of the same dye lot. Estimate your needs and buy that amount or slightly more. Most stores will accept for exchange or return unopened skeins.

The amount of yarn needed to complete a project is determined both by the size of the canvas and the stitches that will be used. For example, to cover one square inch of No. 10 canvas with the half cross-stitch requires one yard of yarn. If the continental or the basket weave is used, 1¼ yards are needed.

To determine yarn quantities, estimate the total square inches of each color. Multiply by the yardage needed per square inch and divide by the inches contained in the skein of yarn.

Blocking

There is a great deal of difference in the much desired "handmade" look and the sloppy "homemade" look so often seen. This is really a shame because in most cases as much work went into the less professional-looking item as into its attractive counterpart. The difference is often the blocking—or lack of it.

Even if you have been able to keep your piece clean and straight while working, it still needs blocking to give it the crisp, new look you want. If you are like most needlepointers, the piece is wrinkled and crushed and very much out of shape.

Blocking will not remove mistakes. It will, however, make the stitches look evener and smoother. Above all, it will restore the canvas to its original condition and correct any stretching that occurred during the working.

The blocking process is a relatively simple one, but one that must be carried out with precision. It is also something that every needlepointer should try at least once, for the experience provides a knowledge of the kind of labor involved and an insight that will be valuable if you later decide to have your needlepoint professionally blocked.

You will need a blocking board and a supply of rust-proof nails or tacks. The tacks can be either aluminum or copper. An old drawing board makes a good blocking board, but a piece of fiberboard or plywood will do nicely. The board must have a smooth surface that you do not mind marring with nail holes and be of a type that the wet needlepoint will not cause to warp.

The outline of the finished needlepoint should be drawn either on the board or on a piece of paper taped to it. The center of each side should be indicated. These will be the first points to be fastened.

Carefully remove the masking tape from the edges of the needlepoint so that you don't take too many canvas threads with it. Turn under the raw edges of the canvas and stitch firmly. If for any reason you do not have a two-inch border of unworked canvas on all sides, you will have to extend the edges by attaching an extension of firm, colorfast fabric. Stitch a double thickness of the fabric to the canvas and make the extension wide enough so that you do not have to put tacks into the worked needlepoint itself.

Find and mark the center of each side of the canvas. Do this by actually counting the mesh. Mark with a thread or waterproof marker.

To be blocked, the needlepoint must be dampened. To insure that both the canvas and the yarn are completely and evenly damp, roll the piece in a thoroughly moistened towel and leave it overnight. The towel should be very wet but not dripping and of course only cold water is to be used.

When the needlepoint is removed from the towel, it will be very limp. The sizing in the canvas is wet and the needlepoint is pliable and more amenable to the stretching. When dry the sizing will return to its original crispness.

Pulling the canvas as tightly as possible, tack the marked centers of the sides of the canvas to the center marks on the blocking board. Working outward from these points, tack the canvas at one-inch intervals along the edges until you have tacked all four sides completely. This is usually easiest to do if you tack a few points on one side, turn the board, place a few tacks opposite those tacks, and continue until the canvas is fastened. If the canvas is stubborn, do not be afraid to pull. The canvas was strong to begin with and you have added the strength of the yarn.

In many cases, especially in pieces worked in the continental stitch, one corner is very crooked. It may be necessary to move the tacks several times before you are able to work the piece into a straight position on the board. The canvas will stay wet and pliable long enough for you to tack and retack, if necessary.

Sometimes a needlepoint piece is very much out of shape. This is usually the result of the stitches having been worked too tightly. In these cases it seems that the canvas will never be straight. If this happens, tack the piece into place as nearly straight as possible and leave to dry. Redampen and repeat the blocking process. The second time is not nearly as much trouble as the first and is definitely worthwhile. Some badly misshapen pieces may need to be blocked two or three times.

The needlepoint must stay on the blocking board until it is completely dry. The board should lie flat and should never be placed near heat or in direct sunlight. The time needed for drying will, of course, vary with the weather conditions. Don't try to shorten the drying time by removing the needlepoint from the board while wet. The canvas will return to its unblocked shape.

Keep in mind that blocking is the only method for straightening needlepoint. You cannot correct a crooked piece by sewing or mounting. A pillow that starts out as a misshapen piece of needlepoint will always have an odd shape.

Needlepoint cannot be successfully blocked with the steam iron. The canvas must dry in the straightened position and there is no practical way to accomplish this with the steam iron. Never press your needlepoint with the iron. The stitches will be mashed flat and distorted. There may, however, be times when the needlepoint needs only a little freshening. This can be done by holding the iron above the needlepoint and allowing the steam to penetrate the yarn. The iron should never be allowed to rest on the needlepoint.

Finishing and mounting

It is not the purpose of this book to go into the exact sewing and mounting techniques in detail. There are a few general rules that will interest most readers.

Some projects are easily finished at home with only a little basic knowledge of sewing and construction. These are the smaller, easy to handle items such as pillows, belts, pin cushions. tote bags, eyeglass cases, slip seats, book covers, bookends, and doorstops. It is safe to assume that if the project is one that you would attempt to make from a fine fabric, you will be successful in making it from your needlepoint. Basically, needlepoint is a fine quality, but heavy fabric and should be handled as such.

7 Projects and directions

This section contains black and white pictures, charts, and directions for making the pillows shown in color on pages 36 to 38. These pictures and the detailed, ready-to-work graphed charts mean that you can get right to work.

Floral ribbon pillow

The Ute and Ojibwa floral designs on pages 31 and 32 are examples of the delicate trend in later Indian beadwork. Their colorings and placement on the pages suggest using them ribbon-fashion on a pillow. Spacing and centering the designs was easy for this had already been done on the bead charts. Colors were used just as they appear on the charts; the only modification required was the addition of the center blue flower in the top "ribbon." This addition made the design wide enough to fit the space needed by the other bands.

An easy border outlines each "ribbon" as well as the outside edges of the pillow. The colors of the pillow are those of the bead charts—bright red, yellow, blue, green, and white. The pillow was worked on No. 14 mesh white mono canvas with two-ply Persian yarn. It measures 11 inches by 12½ inches.

Don't overlook the many possible uses for these flower designs, including cross-stitch embroidery on a variety of items. The detail shows a portion of one band worked on Hardanger cloth with two strands of cotton embroidery floss. The stitch here is the half cross and the effect is that of petit point.

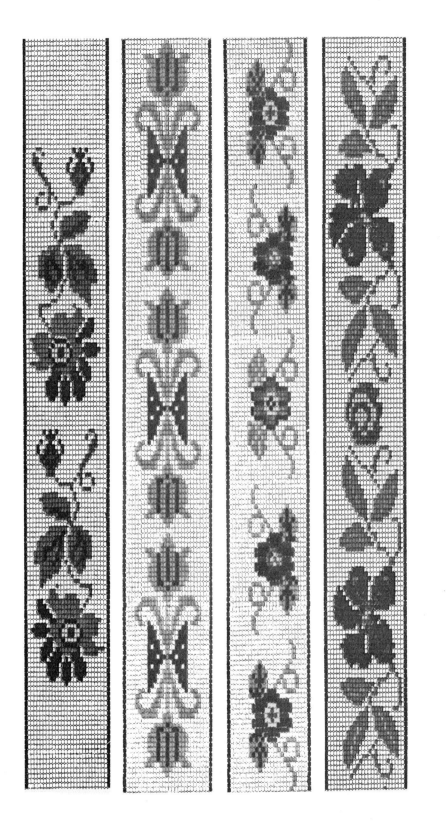

Chart 3
Floral ribbon pillow

Sioux mountain-lake-rainbow pillow and bell pull

This pair would be a gay addition to any room. Both were worked on No. 13 mesh beige mono canvas with two-ply Persian yarn in the colors of the bead charts on page 25. The colors are bright shades of red, orange, yellow, navy, green, black, and white.

For the bell pull, the mountain-lake strip was reproduced for the center of the panel exactly as it appears on the bead chart. The rainbow pattern, lying above it on the page, seemed perfect for the border. On the right side it was used just as it appears; on the left side it was reversed to make a pleasing composition. The point at the bottom of the bell pull was a natural outgrowth of the design itself. Finishing with the big fluffy tassel was fun and less formal than using conventional bell pull hardware.

The difference in the depth of the mountain and lake motifs presented a design problem and necessitated laying out the design on graph paper. The solution was reached by reducing in length the mountain symbols in the two side panels. Graphing the design also simplified laying out the rainbows in a logical manner. Trimming the pillow with the dozen little tassels makes it match the bell pull without being a duplicate.

Chart 4
Sioux mountain-lake-rainbow pillow and bell pull

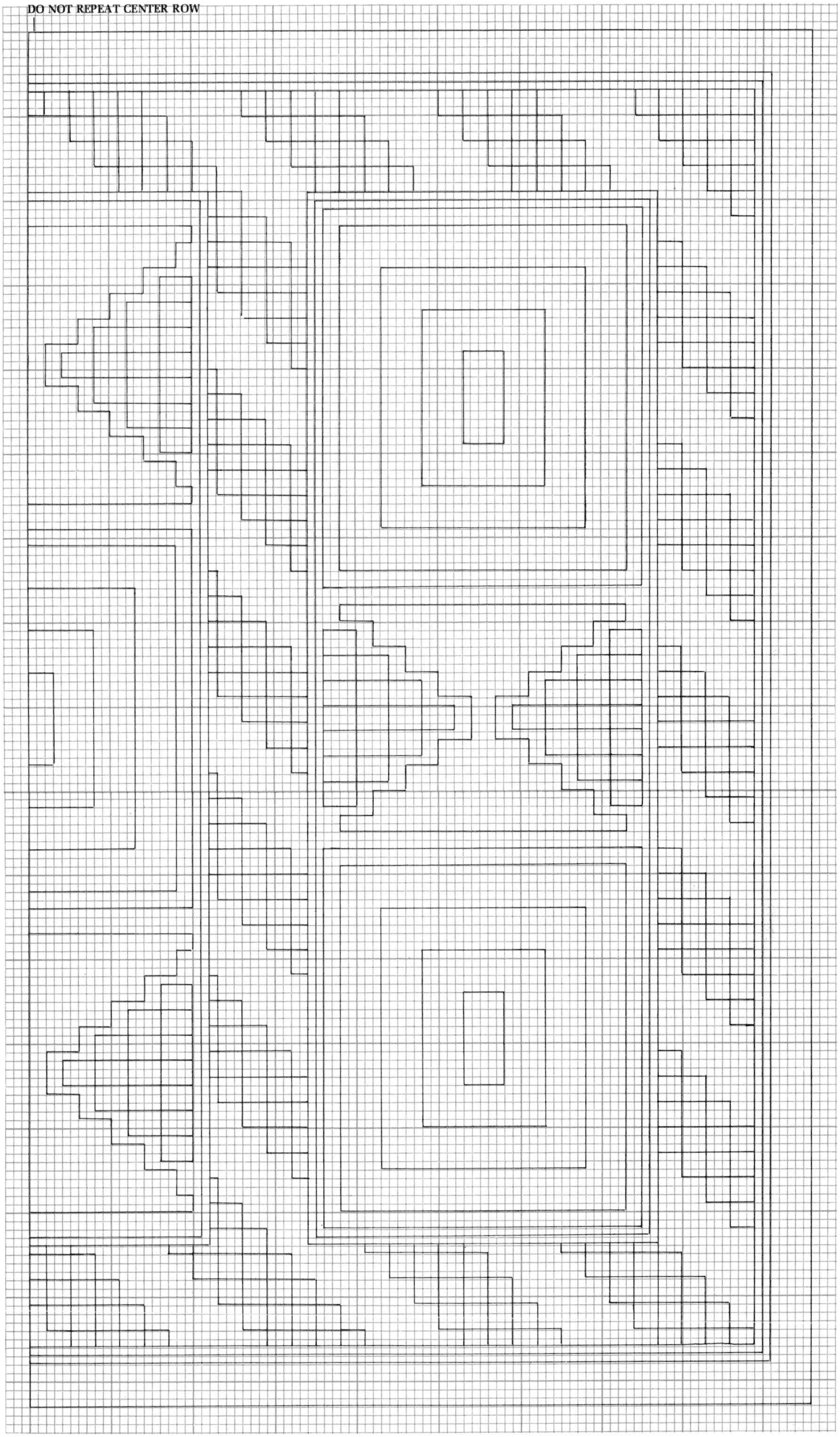
DO NOT REPEAT CENTER ROW

Ojibwa pillow

The colorful design for this pillow came from the Ojibwa beaded bandoleer bag embroidered in the appliqué method pictured below. To duplicate the appearance of the beading, the entire design was worked in the couching stitch. The rows of couching were laid on the canvas following the lines of the beading as closely as possible. The result is surprisingly like the original.

The pillow was worked on No. 12 mesh white mono canvas using three-ply Persian yarn except for the tie-down couching thread which was single ply. The background is upright gobelin, and it should be mentioned that the best results will be obtained if the background is worked before the design is embroidered. The upright gobelin stitches should be worked so that they extend slightly into the outlines of the flowers. The first row of couching will then be laid on top so that all canvas is covered.

The pillow border is composed of four rows of the upright gobelin stitch picking up colors from the design. The first row is light green worked over two threads. The second row is four threads wide in orange and white alternating two white stitches with eight orange. The third row is also four threads wide with six yellow stitches centered over the two white of the previous row while four orange stitches fill in. A row of light green four threads wide completes the border pattern. To fill in the spaces between the rows of gobelin stitches in the border, a row of back stitches in a matching color has been used.

The pillow measures 12 inches by 12 inches.

Chart 5
Ojibwa pillow

Acoma pillow

This pillow, featuring a relatively simple Acoma motif, is included in this collection to point out the wide variety of Indian designs that adapt naturally to needlepoint. Designs can be found in rugs, pottery, sand paintings, jewelry, and ceremonial masks as well as beadwork.

This little pillow, which measures 11 inches by 11 inches, is worked in the beige and brown of much American Indian pottery on No. 12 mesh mono canvas using two-ply Persian yarn. A simple striped border finishes the pillow.

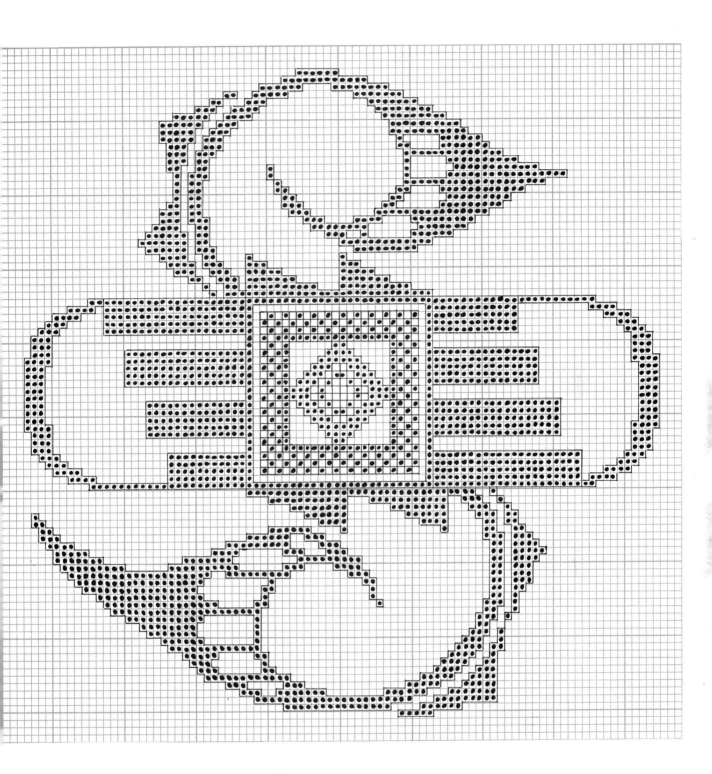

Chart 6
Acoma pillow

Blue-brown Sioux pillow

This handsome geometric design is taken from the Sioux armband next to the bottom on page 35. The design was repeated three times to form a square shape. Though the colors have been changed to pale blues and four shades of brown the feeling remains Indian. A border of blue and brown unifies the strips into a single design unit.

Chart 7 shows one quarter of the pillow. This model was worked on No. 10 mesh white mono canvas with three-ply Persian yarn in the basket weave stitch. The finished pillow measures 12 inches by 13 inches. The colors used are pale blue, medium blue, Indian pink, light rust, rust, and brown. This kind of design worked on rug canvas would make a striking floor pillow.

PALE BLUE   LIGHT RUST

— MEDIUM BLUE   · RUST

/ INDIAN PINK   ● BROWN

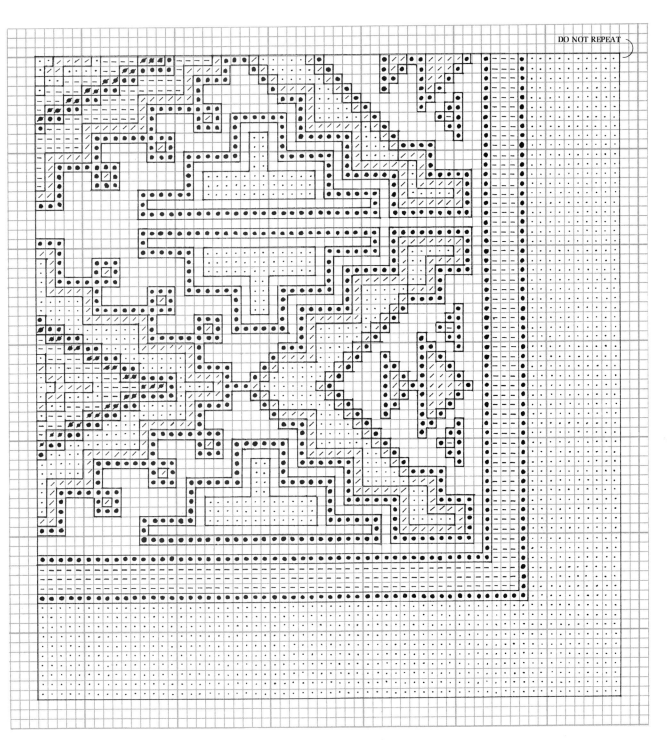

DO NOT REPEAT

Chart 7
Blue-brown Sioux pillow

69

Sioux geometric pillow

Three repeats of the Sioux armband (see bottom of page 35) produced this gay pillow. The colors are taken directly from the chart; the only alteration is the addition of small motifs at the end of the strip to widen it slightly—the tails of the arrows are longer and the remaining spaces are filled in with small rectangles of red, yellow, and green. The addition of the border ties the three strips into a square design.

The pillow was worked with three-ply Persian yarn on No. 10 mesh white mono canvas. It measures approximately 12 inches by 13 inches. The colors used are bright blue, navy, kelly green, true red, yellow, and white. Chart 8 shows one quarter of the pillow. Note that the center rows of the chart—both horizontal and vertical—should not be repeated.

Most of the geometric band designs can be repeated in the same manner to create square or oblong shapes. Block the first one roughly on graph paper before beginning to work. With practice you will be able to work right from the bead charts. Remember, also, that a border or series of borders is very handy for tieing together a design as well as enlarging a piece.

WEDGEWOOD BLUE   / SCARLET

● NAVY   ⚡ YELLOW

□ WHITE   ~ KELLY GREEN

DO NOT REPEAT

DO NOT REPEAT

Chart 8
Sioux geometric pillow

Navajo pillow

This pillow and its mate, the lake Indian pillow on page 76, are worked in lovely Indian colors not usually associated with beaded designs. The yarns used were two-ply Persian in Indian pink, light rust, rust, light turquoise, medium turquoise, dark turquoise, yellow, and black. The pillow measures 11 inches by 17 inches.

The center panel of the pillow was taken bead by bead from the loomed-beaded Navajo bag pictured below. The design for the bag itself came originally from a Navajo rug.

Following the current trend of combining several patterns into one design, two narrow plain and two patterned borders have been added to enlarge the center panel into a more interesting shape. The motifs in the smaller of the patterned borders are two miscellaneous shapes that could be arranged easily to fit the dimensions while the wider patterned edge was created by taking an important motif from the center of the rug and spacing it carefully around the edges of the pillow. Working out this kind of border so that the design is centered and turns corners correctly often requires much drawing and planning, but the result is definitely worthwhile.

● BLACK

／ RUST

· LIGHT RUST

〓 LIGHT TURQUOISE

– INDIAN PINK

✓ YELLOW

∨ MEDIUM TURQUOISE

✕ DARK TURQUOISE

Chart 9
Navajo pillow

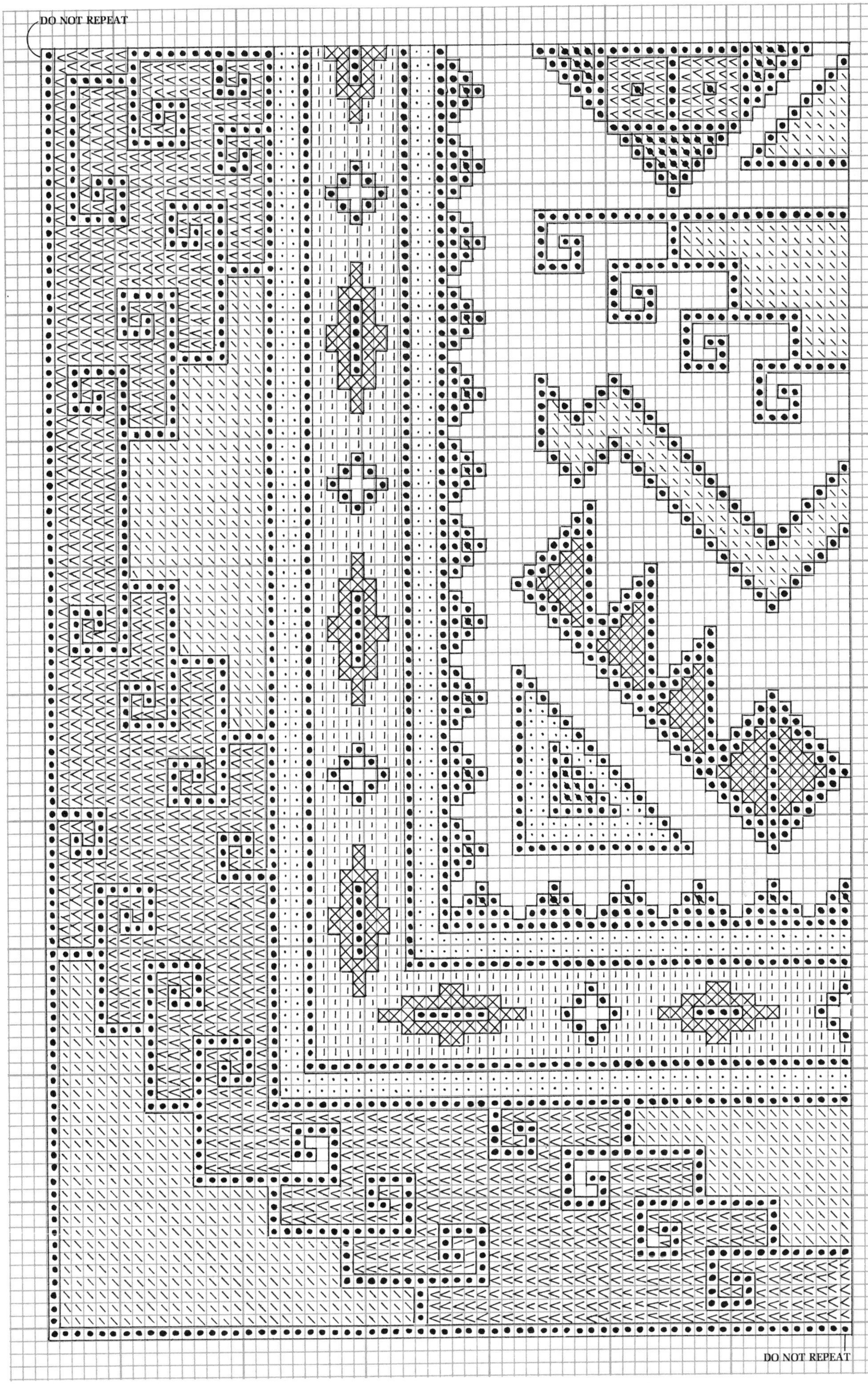
DO NOT REPEAT
DO NOT REPEAT

Sioux "T" necklace

Just for fun needlepoint was used to create a choker like those shown below. These necklaces are still being made and sold by the Indians and, of course, there is nothing like the real thing, but this one will be an unusual accessory and certainly a conversation piece.

The design came from the Sioux design on page 35 and the colors used are those of the original beadwork— blue, yellow, red, green, and white. The chart shows one half of the necklace. The canvas used was No. 14 mesh penelope, and it was worked with six-strand embroidery floss. This produced a piece of needlepoint without bulk which would be uncomfortable and too stiff to be attractive.

To finish the necklace in the Indian manner, a fringe of seed beads was added at the lower edge. At each side of the center panel hang two strings of seed beads.

● BLUE

⚡ YELLOW

／ RED

• GREEN

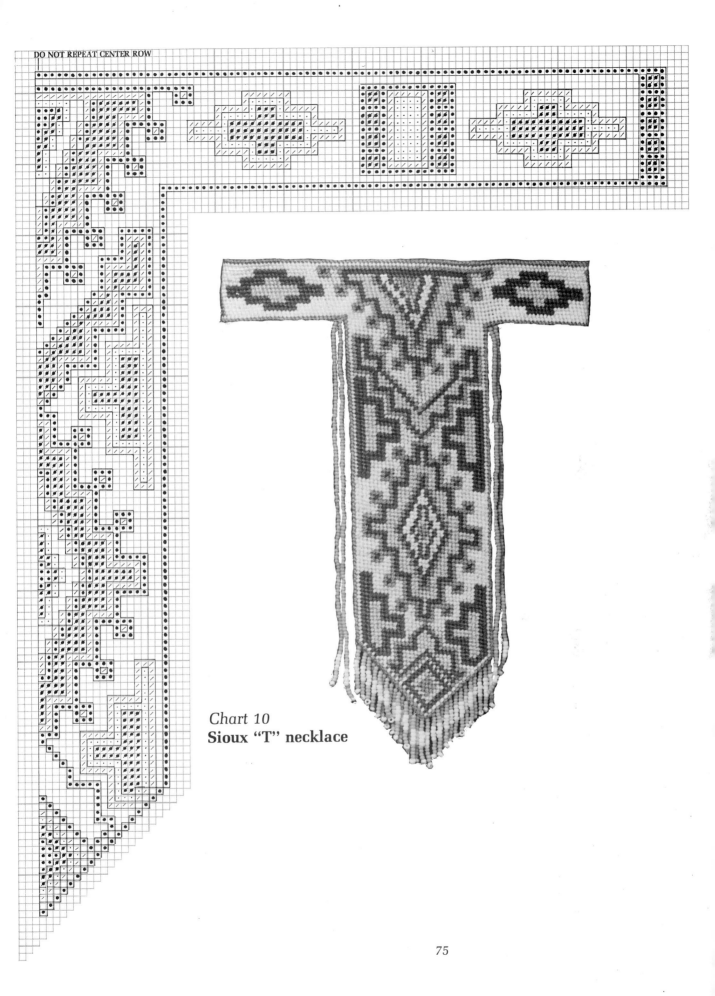

DO NOT REPEAT CENTER ROW

Chart 10
Sioux "T" necklace

Lake Indian pillow

One motif from the lake Indian floral abstract on page 29 was redrawn to form the center of this unusual pillow. Since the motif was not square, it was laid out on graph paper and slightly altered. To fill in the empty spaces caused by the recharting a few small symbols were added along the edges.

The small inside border contains two miniature symbols that were spaced evenly around the square to add pattern without clashing. The outside border was taken from an armband on page 27. Small liberties were taken at each corner, and the lozenge was added between the motifs to make the border fit.

The colors in this pillow and its mate, the Navajo pillow on page 72, are lovely Indian colors not usually found in beadwork. They are Indian pink, light rust, rust, light turquoise, medium turquoise, dark turquoise, yellow, and black. Worked on No. 12 mesh white mono canvas with two-ply Persian yarn, it measures 13½ inches by 13½ inches.

● BLACK   ✎ YELLOW

/ RUST   — LIGHT TURQUOISE

· LIGHT RUST   V MEDIUM TURQUOISE

□ INDIAN PINK   X DARK TURQUOISE

Chart 11
Lake Indian pillow

Ojibwa quill-decorated armband

An Ojibwa quill-embroidered armband just 1½ inches wide yields this beautiful design. Using one upright gobelin stitch in place of one quill produces a motif 5 inches wide. The worked detail of the piece shows only the two primary design sections. The needlepoint was worked in Indian red, black, and white on No. 14 mesh white mono canvas. Several repeats of this pattern would make a beautiful pillow. The same design and colors worked on large mesh rug canvas would be a striking rug or wall hanging.

Chart 12
Ojibwa quill-decorated armband

Sioux saddlebag pillow

The design for this pillow came from the saddlebag on page 34. Design and colors are exactly as shown in the chart. The pillow is worked in quickpoint on rug canvas with a double strand of knitting worsted. It measures 12 inches by 18 inches. The difference in the oblong shape of the beads and the square needlepoint stitches accounts for the variance in the shape of the pillow and the chart.

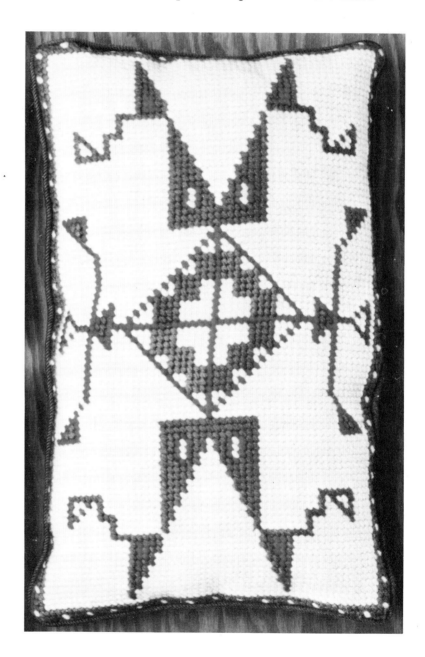

8 Projects to make using needlepoint

The following is a list of projects you can make yourself.

Home decorating

Book covers
Book marks
Chair seats
Christmas ornaments
Church kneelers
Clock faces
Coasters
Director's chairs
Dolls and toys
Door stops
Drapery tie-backs
Fire screens
Game boards
Lamp bases
Luggage rack straps

Mirror and picture borders
Napkin rings
Parsons tables
Pictures
Pillows
Pin cushions
Rugs
Screen Panels
Tea cozies
Tray inserts
Trivets
Typewriter covers
Valances
Wall hangings and tapestries

Personal accessories

Armbands and bracelets
Belts
Cosmetic cases
Desk sets
Eyeglass cases
Golf mitts
Guitar straps
Handbags
Hats and caps
Head bands
Jewelry rolls

Key and luggage tags
Needle books
Pockets
Scissors case
Slippers
Tennis racket covers
Ties
Tote bags
Vests
Wallets

Index